'Know the Game' Series

LAWN TENNIS

CONTENTS

Foreword

This booklet makes simple and easy in theory what many of us find complex and difficult in practice. It, therefore, deserves the success it has had and will, I hope, continue to have.

To encourage the beginner to start aright is to give him, or her, the chance of that enjoyment, excitement and exercise that comes from playing the game of lawn tennis, whether it is done superbly or not so well. The reader of this booklet will soon find himself drawn into the comradeship and friendliness that flourish in the clubs and competitions devoted to the game, and he is to be envied for the fun that is ahead of him.

I would commend this booklet not only to the beginner, but also to the improving player, as well as to the parent and spectator. It does us all good to learn and to understand.

Good luck !

Carl Aarvold

President,
THE LAWN TENNIS ASSOCIATION.

The Administration of Lawn Tennis

THE Governing Body of the Game in this country, whether amateur or professional, is the Lawn Tennis Association, which operates in the main through a Council composed chiefly of representatives of the Counties of England and the Scottish and Welsh Lawn Tennis Associations. In addition, certain other bodies, such as the All England Club, Wimbledon, Oxford and Cambridge Universities and the Services have direct representation on the Council. Clubs, Schools, Leagues and similar organisations affiliate to the Association of the County in which they are situated. Thus, every Lawn Tennis player, through affiliation with his local Club, Organisation or County, is offered some form of representation on The Lawn Tennis Association.

The main work of the Council of the Association is done by Committees composed of amateur experts in various aspects of the Game and its administration. The Committees report about once a month to a full meeting of the Council, which takes collective responsibility for decisions and which, in turn, reports once a year to a General Meeting of the Association. No alteration to the Rules of the Association can be made except at a General Meeting.

The Governing Body of the Game throughout the world is the International Lawn Tennis Federation which is composed of the National Associations of the various countries. The Rules of the Game, as distinct from administrative rules and regulations, are under the sole authority of the International Federation and are, therefore, standard throughout the world. As a graceful tribute to the country which founded the Game, the International Federation has decreed that " The official and decisive test of the Rules of Lawn Tennis shall be for ever in the English language."

Although a very great deal of honorary work is given each year towards the administration of the Game at various levels, the success of these efforts must depend to a great extent upon the spirit in which the Game is played.

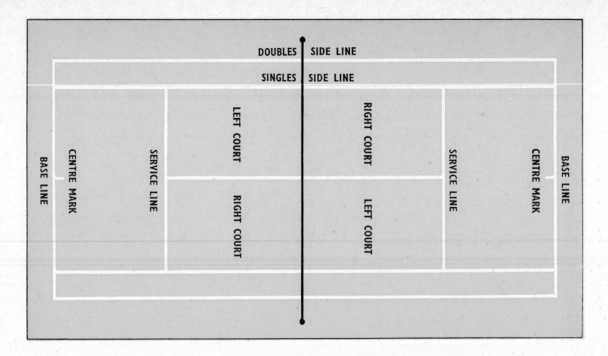

The Court

The Doubles court is larger than the Singles court by 4 ft. 6 ins. (1.37 m.) at each side, popularly known as the "tram lines". It is marked by white lines. Usually of chalk or tape.

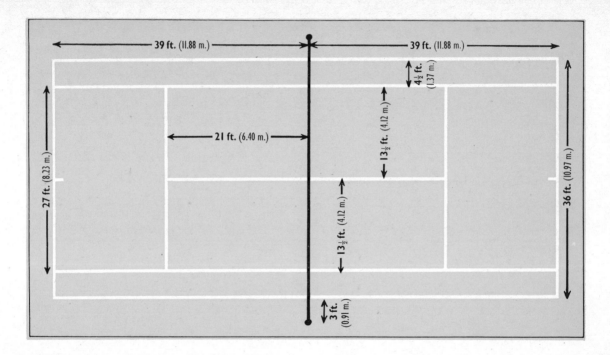

In addition to grass courts there are hard courts with a loose gritty surface which require attention, and non-attention courts with an asphalt surface. Play on grass courts is mostly confined to the summer months when the turf is firm and dry. The loose surface and asphalt courts are all-weather courts and are more suitable to winter conditions.

Equipment

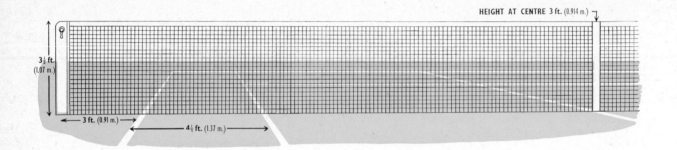

HEIGHT AT CENTRE 3 ft. (0.914 m.)

3½ ft. (1.07 m.)

3 ft. (0.91 m.)

4½ ft. (1.37 m.)

THE NET

It is suspended between two posts from a cord or cable, which is covered by a tape 2—2½ inches (0.05m.—0.063m.) in depth. The net is kept taut at the centre by a strap not more than 2 inches (0.05m.) wide and firmly fixed to the ground. The net height is arranged by winding handles in the posts, the final adjustment being made by a screw on the bottom of the centre strap.

The net should be slackened when play ceases in the evening to reduce the strain on the posts. The bottom of the net should be turned over the net band so that it will not be frayed by wind action in dragging it to and fro across the ground.

THE BALL

Rule 3 defines the weight, size, bound and compression of the ball and stipulates that the outer surface should be uniform and seams, if any, should be stitchless. Balls which have deteriorated through age or have become smooth with much usage are difficult to control. Such ball will make it difficult to maintain accuracy, and so may cause lack of confidence.

THE RACKET

There are no rules affecting the specifications of the racket, but the following suggestions are made to assist in choice.

The usual weight for a man is between $13\frac{1}{2}$ and 14 ozs., for ladies 13 to $13\frac{1}{2}$ ozs. Too light a racket lessens driving power. Smaller, light-weight rackets from 9-11 ozs. are available for juniors.

Balance is a matter of individual choice. Heaviness in the head tends to aid ground shots while lightness tends to aid volleying.

The grip is also a matter of individual choice so long as the racket can be held comfortably. A leather grip provides secure and comfortable hold, although the fingers and thumb should not meet when gripping the racket.

Medium and stout gauge gut will last longer than thin gut, and medium tension stringing is more durable than super tension, which is only suitable for top-grade players; for others it may be a handicap. Nylon is an alternative to gut and it can be used in wet weather.

Keep the racket in a cool, even temperature with the head up. Use a press when the racket is not in play, and preserve it from rain with a waterproof cover, first making sure that the racket is dry. Do not keep the racket in its waterproof cover for long periods.

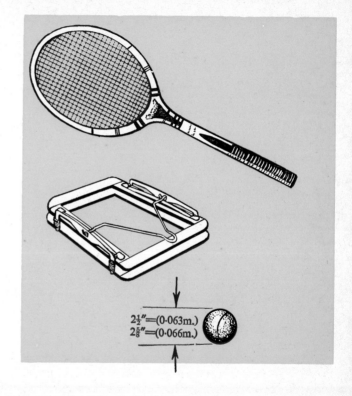

$2\frac{1}{2}'' = (0.063\text{m.})$
$2\frac{5}{8}'' = (0.066\text{m.})$

Dress

Tennis is a fast game and therefore the selection of dress is of vital importance. There is no uniform rule, but white is the accepted wear.

It should be sweat absorbing and should allow the player unrestricted movement.

For men the polo shirt is very popular because it is easily washed, and takes only a few moments to slip on and off. There are two types of shorts, the flannel and the linen drill, both are widely used.

Ladies usually wear absorbent blouses and either skirts or shorts.

Tennis shoes are by far the most important item in a player's dress. They must be heel-less and it is preferable that they should have a toe-cap. Sorbo is now a common type of pad inside the shoe. It is wise as well to have an arch support. This will support and strengthen the instep. When fitting for tennis shoes, make sure that they are a little on the large side because it is wise to play with two pairs of socks.

It is important to wear woollen socks, these absorb the sweat and they do not cake like cotton socks do.

The Singles Game

The game is started by one player serving and the question of which side will serve first and who will have choice of ends is decided by spinning a racket in the air and calling either rough or smooth.

The winner may select one of four alternatives—

(a) Elect to serve—in which case his opponent has choice of ends.

(b) Elect to receive—in which case his opponent has choice of ends.

(c) Choose ends—in which case his opponent may elect to serve or receive.

(d) Request his opponent to make the choice.

The server stands behind the base-line to the right of an imaginary continuation of the centre mark and between this and the singles side line. The receiver takes up any position he thinks most suitable on his own side of the net. The first service is delivered from the right-hand side of the court.

The stroke is completed when the racket touches the ball. The ball served must pass over the net without bouncing, and fall within the service court diagonally opposite the server, or on any of the lines bounding such court (Rule 8). After each point scored by either side the server changes to the other side of the centre mark for his next service, and so on.

On completion of the first game, the player who has been the Receiver becomes the Server in the next game.

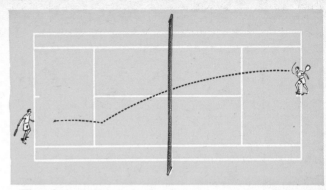

The players then serve in alternate games until the end of the match.

If a player serves out of turn, the player who should have served must serve as soon as the mistake is discovered. All points scored up to this discovery will stand, but a single fault served before the discovery will not be counted. If a game is completed before the discovery is made, the order of service remains as altered.

The players change ends at the conclusion of the first, third and every alternate game until the end of the set. If at the conclusion of the set, the number of games played in that set is even, the players play one more game, i.e., the first game of the next set, before changing ends. When the number of games played in a set is uneven, the players change ends at the conclusion of that set and continue changing at the end of the first, third, fifth, seventh, etc., game until the set is finished (see Scoring page 15).

The Service

In delivering the service the server should : —

(a) Not serve until the receiver is ready. If the receiver is not ready a *let* is called, meaning that the point does not count and the service is taken again.

If, however, the receiver attempts to play the ball he cannot then claim a let for not being ready.

(b) Throw the ball into the air by hand (Rule 6).

(c) Strike the ball with his racket before it reaches the ground. If the server tosses the ball into the air and catches it again it is a *let*. If he makes a stroke but misses the ball completely then it is a *fault*.

(d) Keep both feet behind the base-line, and to the correct side of the centre mark until the ball is hit. If not, it is a *fault*.

(e) Not walk or run whilst delivering the service (Rule 7)—*fault*.

Note: Slight foot movements are permitted and an unrestricted movement of one foot so long as the other maintains contact with the ground.

SERVING OUT OF TURN (Rule 14)

If a player serves out of turn, the player who should have served must serve as soon as the mistake is discovered. All points scored up to this discovery will stand, but a single fault served before the discovery will not be counted. If a game is completed before the discovery is made, the order of the service remains as altered.

FAULTS

If the first service from the correct side is a fault, the server is allowed one more service from the same side.

If the first fault is due to a service from the wrong side, the server may only deliver one more service from the correct side.

If the second service is a fault, making a " double fault," the server loses the point. After a good service play continues until a point is scored by either player.

A service ball striking the net, strap or band and bouncing directly into the correct service court is a "let."

A service ball striking any other fixture other than the net is a fault.

FOOT FAULTS

During the service, if the server touches the base line or the court or stands on the wrong side of the centre mark, a foot fault will be called.

Formerly a fault, but after 1st January, 1959, fair play (See Rule 7).

It is a foot fault if the server touches the line or any other part of the playing area of the court.

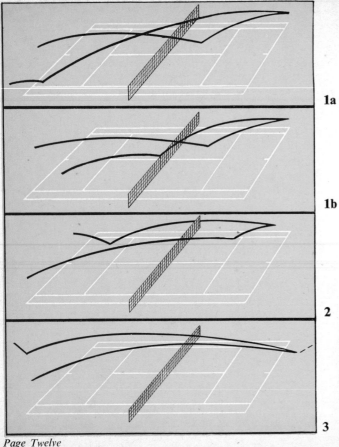

Ball in Play—Returns

1a   1a. A player returns the ball directly into his opponent's court before it bounces twice on his own side of the net. (*Good return.*)

1b. The ball touches the net, post, centre strap, or net band, providing it passes over the net and falls within the opponent's court. (*Good return.*)

2. The ball is returned outside the posts above or below the level of the top of the net and drops within the proper court. (*Good return.*)

1b

3. The server has served the ball. The receiver does not wait for the ball to bounce, but volleys it. (*Loses the point*).

4. He hits the ball more than once in making a stroke, i.e., a double hit. (*Loses the point.*)

2

3   **4**

5

5. The ball bounces back over the net and the player on whose side it bounced reaches over the net and plays the ball (*good return* providing that neither he nor his racket touches the net, post, or ground in his opponent's court).

6. He throws his racket at and hits the ball. (*Loses the point.*)

7. The ball touches him or anything he wears or carries (except his racket) while the ball is in play. (*Loses the point.*)

8. A player strikes the ball before it has crossed the net. (*Loses the point.*)

9. A player succeeds in returning the ball which has struck another ball lying on the court. (*Good return.*)

6

7

8

9

Ball in and out of Play

(Rule 15)

A ball is in play from the moment it is delivered in service (unless a fault or let is given) and remains in play until the point is decided.

BALL TOUCHING PERMANENT FIXTURE

(Rule 21)

If the ball in play, i.e., after the service, touches a permanent fixture (other than the net, posts, centre strap, or net band) before it bounces, the striker loses the point. If it strikes the permanent fixture after it bounces, his opponent loses the point.

BALL IN COURT

(Rule 20)

" A ball falling on a line is regarded as falling in the court bounded by that line." The diagram illustrates the correct interpretation of this rule. On a grass court the chalk is liable to fly, even though the ball may bounce beyond the limits of the court, especially if the surface is worn or dusty. A puff of chalk should therefore not be regarded as conclusive evidence that the ball has touched the line.

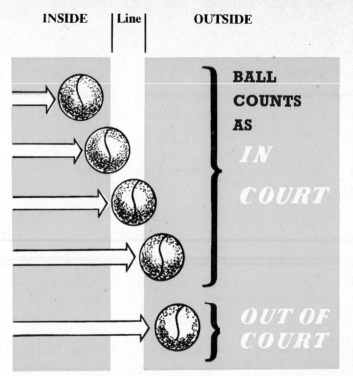

Ball at moment of bounce

Order of Service in a Singles Game (Rule 14)

On completion of the first game, the player who has been the Receiver becomes the Server in the next game. The players then serve in alternate games until the end of the match.

Change of Ends (Rule 26)

The players change ends at the conclusion of the first, third, and every alternate game until the end of the set. If at the conclusion of the set the number of games played in that set is even, the players play one more game, i.e., the first game of the next set, before changing ends. When the number of games played in a set is uneven, the players change ends at the conclusion of that set and continue changing at the end of the first, third, fifth, seventh, etc., game until the set is finished (see Scoring).

Scoring

GAME

The first point any player (or pair in doubles) wins is called 15. The second point to the same player or pair is called 30, the third point is called 40 and the fourth point is called GAME. The server's score is always given first. If A is serving to B and wins the first point the score is Fifteen-Love (i.e., 15 to A, and 0 to B). If B wins the first point the score is Love-Fifteen (i.e., 0 to A and 15 to B). When both players have won a point the score is Fifteen All (i.e., 15 to A, and 15 to B) and so on.

DEUCE

If the opponents score three points each (i.e., 40 to A, and 40 to B) the score is called "Deuce". In this case A or B must win two consecutive points to score game. If A wins the next point the score is "advantage server" or "advantage in ", A being the server. If B wins the point the score is "advantage striker" or "advantage out". Should the score be "deuce" and A wins the next point ("advantage in") and loses the following point, the score becomes "deuce" again, and so on until either A or B lead by two points to win the game.

SET

The first player or pair to win six games wins the set, except that should the score become five games each— "Five All"—one player or pair must become two games ahead to win the set.

MATCH

The maximum number of sets in a match is 5, or where women take part is three. Local Tournament Rules usually stipulate the number of sets to be played in a match, but normally, matches are decided on the best of three sets.

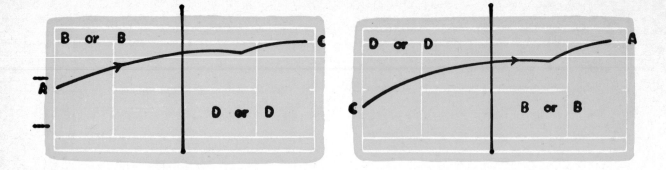

The Doubles Game

The court dimensions for Doubles are shown on page 4. Service and choice of ends are decided by tossing or calling as in the Singles game (page 9.)

ORDER OF SERVICE

The pair serving first must decide which partner will serve in the opening game. The opposing pairs decide who will serve in the second game. Supposing A and B win the toss and choose to serve. If A decides to serve in the opening game and C chooses to serve in the second game, B will serve in the third game, and D in the fourth game. A serves again in the fifth game and service continues A, C, B, D, A, C, B, D, etc., until the set is ended. At the beginning of a new set the order may be changed if desired, but not during a set.

SERVING OUT OF TURN

If a player serves out of turn his partner who ought to have served must serve as soon as the mistake is discovered, but any points scored and any fault served before the discovery will stand. If a game is completed

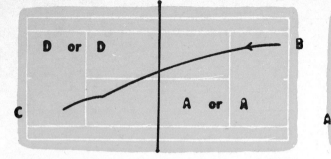 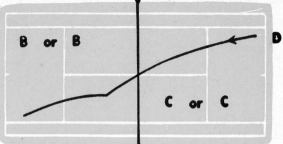

before the mistake is discovered, the order of serving will remain as altered.

The server stands behind the base-line between an imaginary continuation of the centre mark and the doubles side-line (outer tram-line).

ORDER OF RECEIVING SERVICE

Partners must decide who is to receive in the right court and who in the left. Once they have received in those courts, they cannot change until the start of a new set. As C receives in the right court in the diagram he will continue to do so until the end of the set.

ERROR IN ORDER OF RECEIVING

If a player receives in the wrong court, he continues in that court until the end of the game but reverts to his correct court in the next receiving game of that set. There is no rule requiring the player who receives first in the first game to serve in the second game. Although C chooses to receive in the first, either of the pair may be the first to serve, but will commence serving from the right side. C can serve in the second or fourth game. Once this order of service has been established, it must be kept throughout the set, i.e., A, D, B, C, etc.

BALL TOUCHING SERVER'S PARTNER

The service is a fault if the ball touches the server's partner or anything which she wears or carries.

BALL TOUCHING RECEIVER'S PARTNER

If the service is otherwise good but the ball touches the receiver's partner or anything he wears or carries, either before or after bouncing, the server scores the point.

Match Play

UMPIRE'S DECISION FINAL

When there is an umpire, his decision is final on all questions of fact. Appeal to the referee (if there is one) can only be allowed on questions of law.

A linesman is responsible for line and his decision is final. If either umpire or linesman give an erroneous decision and then corrects himself the point must be replayed.

POSTPONEMENT OF MATCHES

The referee may postpone matches on account of darkness, or the condition of the court or the weather. When a match is postponed the players will resume on the same court and continue the score from the point of interruption unless the referee and the players unanimously agree otherwise.

PLAY SHALL BE CONTINUOUS

Play must be continuous from the first service until the match is concluded. Play can never be suspended, delayed or interrupted for the purpose of enabling a player to recover his strength or to receive advice. In the case of Davis or Wightman Cup matches, a special exception is made to permit an interval of ten minutes after the third set for men and the second set for women players.

The Grips

FOREHAND GRIP (Eastern)

This grip is used by most players solely for the Forehand Drive. You clasp the racket as if you were shaking hands with it so that the side of the handle actually digs in between the thumb and forefinger, and the back of the handle and the palm of the hand are in one plane.

The weight of the wrist is behind the racket and it is this which enables the player to obtain power of stroke.

Forehand Grip

Forehand Grip

BACKHAND GRIP

From the Forehand Grip the hand shifts to the left, bringing the palm of the hand more on top of the handle, while the thumb is usually placed diagonally across the back of the handle.

SERVICE GRIP

This is between the Forehand and Backhand grips and is called the CHOPPER, because the head of the racket is in the same relation to the hand as in a chopper when cutting wood. This grip is also used for volleys.

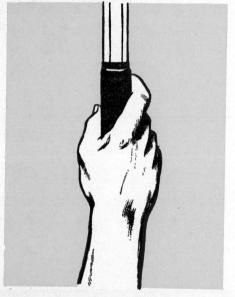

Backhand Grip

Backhand Grip

The Service

1. It is said that a server relies on rhythm. This means that the service involves perfect co-ordination of hands and body.

2. Here the knees are bent with the weight on the toes. The eyes are on the ball and the body leans back. Left hand has risen well above the head to release the ball.

3. The weight of the body is just starting to come forward and upward. Racket head will drop down and away from the body.

4. Most of the weight is on the left foot. The knees are straightening and the racket head has come up from below the wrist.

5. The right leg comes forward to allow body pivot. The left leg has straightened. Racket arm is at full stretch. Eyes on the ball which is just wide of the shoulder.

6. This is the complete follow-through. The right leg has followed through with the rest of the body, but not across the left leg.

Forehand Drive

1. **Watch** the ball leaving your opponent's racket and begin to prepare your stroke by turning sideways and taking your racket back in normal groove.

2. Note the forward sway of body and the bending of the knees. See the eyes are on the ball.

3. The body is moving in to the stroke. Hand and racket will fall in completing loop.

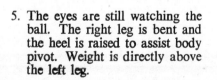

4. The weight is now on the front foot, with the body leaning on to it. Loop has been completed and racket will swing out wide from the body.

5. The eyes are still watching the ball. The right leg is bent and the heel is raised to assist body pivot. Weight is directly above the left leg.

6. Now this is the follow-through of the racket. Notice the straight lean through with the stroke. The legs are straightening out so that he will be ready for his next stroke.

Backhand Drive

1. The preparation, by pronounced turn of body. Toes pointing to tramlines.

2. Racket and arm pass back to left side of the body. Right foot moving forward with sway of the body.

3. Notice the distribution of weight on the right foot as racket swings out from the body.

4. Here the body is all on the right foot with the weight coming up and forward. Notice the firmness of the wrist. The body is well balanced with tendency to lean into the ball.

5. The ball has left the racket but the body and the racket are still following through. Note the swivel of the body comes from the knees and not from the waist.

6. This is the completion of the stroke. Note the perfect balance maintained. The eyes follow the flight of the ball.

Forehand Volley

1. This shows the volley taken on the run and demands mental alertness of the player together with agile footwork.

2. The body is swinging forward to meet the ball after turning sideways with feet pointing to tramlines. Racket is lifted above point of intended contact.

3. The Impact. Racket face is bevelled back. Right leg moving up to left will bring body weight forward.

Low Backhand Volley

1. The player has anticipated the return and is moving into position to volley. Both hands controlling the racket.

2. The whole body is moving forward into the stroke with the right leg taking the weight.

3. Finish of stroke. The power is obtained by the body meeting the ball and not by the swinging of the arm.

The Smash

1. The secret of smashing well is to have perfect footwork bringing the player directly under the ball.

2. All the weight is on the rear foot. It is most important that the body should be sideways to the net. The left hand rises and points at the ball.

3. The player has jumped for this stroke, stretching the body to the utmost.

4. See the racket dropping behind the wrist as with the service; this is to add to the power of the shot. The whole body will pivot towards the net.

5. The racket is following through. The left foot has come down to the ground. The right foot is swinging up.

6. The finish of the stroke. Often it is not the powerful smash that is the winner, but the carefully placed one deep to the base line or acutely angled.

Practising

Here are four illustrations suggesting good methods of practising strokes.

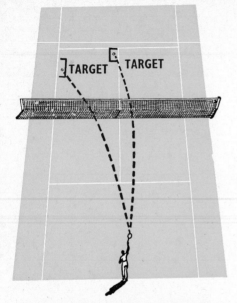

PRACTISING THE SERVICE

Balls should be served repeatedly at targets placed close to the centre line and side line, to get accuracy in the service.

PRACTISING THE VOLLEY

One player drives and the other volleys repeatedly.

PRACTISING THE DRIVE—FOREHAND AND BACKHAND

Repetition of forehand and backhand drive across court and down the line.

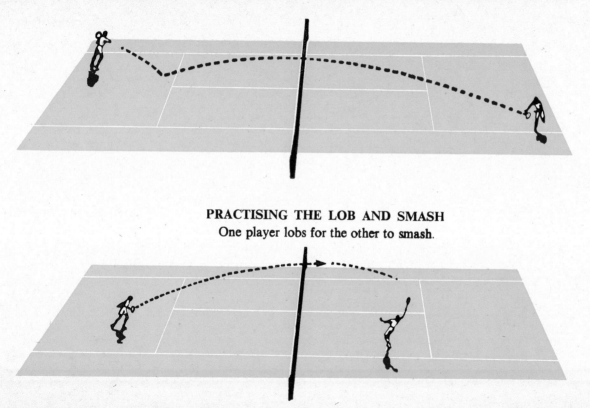

PRACTISING THE LOB AND SMASH

One player lobs for the other to smash.

The Rules of Lawn Tennis

(as approved by the International Lawn Tennis Federation, 1972)

THE SINGLES GAME

1. The Court shall be a rectangle 78 feet (23.77m.) long and 27 feet (8.23m.) wide. It shall be divided across the middle by a net suspended from a cord or metal cable of a maximum diameter of 1/3rd of an inch (0.8 cm.), the ends of which shall be attached to, or pass over, the tops of two evenly painted posts, 3 feet 6 inches (1.07m.) high, and not more than 6 inches (15 cm.) square or 6 inches (15 cm.) in diameter, the centre of which shall be 3 feet (0.91m.) outside the Court on each side. The net shall be extended fully so that it fills completely the space between the two posts and shall be of sufficiently small mesh to prevent the ball passing through. The height of the net shall be 3 feet (0.914m.) at the centre, where it shall be held down taut by a strap not more than 2 inches (5cm.) wide and completely white in colour. There shall be a band covering the cord or metal cable and the top of the net for not less than 2 inches (5cm.) nor more than 2½ inches (6.3cm.) in depth on each side and completely white in colour. There shall be no advertisement on the net, strap, band or singles sticks.

NOTE—In the case of the International Lawn Tennis Championship (Davis Cup) or other Official Championships of the International Federation there shall be a space behind each base-line of not less than 21 feet (6.4m.) and at the sides of not less than 12 feet (3.66m.).

2. The permanent fixtures of the Court shall include not only the net, posts, cord or metal cable, strap and band, but also, where there are any such, the back and side stops, the stands, fixed or movable seats and chairs round the Court, and their occupants, all other fixtures around and above the Court, and the Umpire, Net-cord Judge, Foot-fault Judge, Linesmen and Ball Boys when in their respective places.

NOTE—For the purpose of this Rule, the word "Umpire" comprehends the Umpire, the persons entitled to a seat on the Court, and all those persons designated to assist the Umpire in the conduct of a match.

3. The ball shall have a uniform outer surface and shall be white or yellow in colour. If there are any seams they shall be stitchless. The ball shall be more than two and a half inches (6.35 cm.) and less than two and five-eighths inches (6.67cm.) in diameter, and more than two ounces (56.7 grams) and less than two and one-sixteenth ounces (58.5 grams) in weight. The ball shall have a bound of more than 53 inches (135cm.) and less than 58 inches (147cm.) when dropped 100 inches (254 cm.) upon a concrete base. The ball shall have a forward deformation of more than .220 of an inch (.56cm.) and less thsn .290 of an inch (.74cm.) and a return deformation of more than .350 of an inch (.89cm.) and less than .425 of an inch (1.08cm.) at 18 lb. (8.165kg.) load. The two deformation figures shall be the averages of three individual readings along three axes of the ball and no two individual readings shall differ by more than .03 of an inch (.08cm.) in each case. All tests for bound, size and deformation shall be made in accordance with Regulations in the official Rule Book.

4. The players shall stand on opposite sides of the net; the player who first delivers the ball shall be called the Server, and the other the Receiver.

5. The choice of sides and the right to be Server or Receiver in the first game shall be decided by toss. The player winning the toss may choose or require his opponent to choose:

(a) The right to be Server or Receiver, in which case the other player shall choose the side; or

(b) The side, in which case the other player shall choose the right to be Server or Receiver.

6. The service shall be delivered in the following manner. Immediately before commencing to serve, the Server shall stand with both feet at rest behind (i.e. further from the net than) the base-line, and within the imaginary continuations of the centre-mark and side-line. The Server then shall project the ball by hand into the air in any direction and before it hits the ground strike it with his racket, and the delivery shall be deemed to have been completed at the moment of the impact of the racket and the ball. A player with the use of only one arm may utilize his racket for the projection.

7. The Server shall throughout the delivery of the service:

(a) Not change his position by walking or running.

(b) Not touch, with either foot, any area other than that behind the base-line within the imaginary extension of the centre mark and side-line.

NOTE—The following interpretation of Rule 7 was approved by the International Federation on 9th July, 1958:

7. (a) The Server shall not, by slight movements of the feet which do not materially affect the location originally taken up by him, be deemed "to change his position by walking or running."

(b) The word "foot" means the extremity of the leg below the ankle.

8. (a) In delivering the service, the Server shall stand alternately behind the right and left Courts, beginning from the right in every game. If service from a wrong half of the Court occurs and is undetected, all play resulting from such wrong service or services shall stand, but the inaccuracy of station shall be corrected immediately it is discovered.

(b) The ball served shall pass over the net and hit the ground within the Service Court which is diagonally opposite, or upon any line bounding such Court, before the Receiver returns it.

9. The Service is a fault: (a) If the Server commit any breach of Rules 6, 7 or 8; (b) If he miss the ball in attempting to strike it; (c) If the ball served touch a permanent fixture (other than the net, strap or band) before it hits the ground.

10. After a fault (if it be the first fault) the Server shall serve again from behind the same half of the Court from which he served that fault, unless the service was from the wrong half, when, in accordance with Rule 8, the Server shall be entitled to one service only from behind the other half. A fault may not be claimed after the next service has been delivered.

11. The Server shall not serve until the Receiver is ready. If the latter attempt to return the service, he shall be deemed ready. If, however, the Receiver signify that he is not ready, he may not claim a fault because the ball does not hit the ground within the limits fixed for the service.

12. In all cases where a let has to be called under the rules, or to provide for an interruption to play, it shall have the following interpretations:

(a) When called solely in respect of a service, that one service only shall be replayed.

(b) When called under any other circumstances, the point shall be replayed.

13. The service is a let:

(a) If the ball served touch the net, strap or band, and is otherwise good, or after touching the net, strap or band, touch the Receiver or anything which he wears or carries before hitting the ground.

(b) If a service or fault be delivered when the Receiver is not ready (see Rule 11).

In case of a let, that particular service shall not count, and the Server shall serve again, but a service let does not annul a previous fault.

14. At the end of the first game the Receiver shall become Server, and the Server, Receiver; and so on alternately in all the subsequent games of a match. If a player serve out of turn, the player who ought to have served shall serve as soon as the mistake is discovered, but all points scored before such discovery shall be reckoned. If a game shall have been completed before such discovery, the order of service remains as altered. A fault served before such discovery shall not be reckoned

15. A ball is in play from the moment at which it is delivered in service. Unless a fault or a let be called it remains in play until the point is decided.

16. The Server wins the point:

(a) If the ball served, not being a let under Rule 13, touch the Receiver or anything which he wears or carries, before it hits the ground;

(b) If the Receiver otherwise loses the point as provided by Rule 18.

17. The Receiver wins the point (a) If the Server serve two consecutive faults;

(b) If the Server otherwise lose the point as provided by Rule 18.

18. A player loses the point if:

(a) He fail, before the ball in play has hit the ground twice consecutively, to return it directly over the net (except as provided in Rule 22 (a) or (c); or

(b) He returns the ball in play so that it hits the ground, a permanent fixture, or other object, outside any of the lines which bound his opponent's Court (except as provided in Rule 22 (a) and (c); or

(c) He volley the ball and fail to make a good return even when standing outside the Court; or

(d) He touch or strike the ball in play with his racket more than once in making a stroke; or

(e) He or his racket (in his hand or otherwise) or anything which he wears or carries touch the net, posts, cord or metal cable, strap or band, or the ground within his opponent's Court at any time while the ball is in play; or

(f) He volley the ball before it has passed the net; or

(g) The ball in play touch him or anything that he wears or carries, except his racket in his hand or hands; or

(h) He throws his racket at and hits the ball.

19.　If a player commits any act either deliberately or involuntary which, in the opinion of the Umpire, hinders his opponent in making a stroke, the Umpire shall in the first case award the point to the opponent, and in the second case order the point to be replayed.

20.　A ball falling on a line is regarded as falling in the Court bounded by that line.

21.　If the ball in play touch a permanent fixture (other than the net, posts, cord or metal cable, strap or band) after it has hit the ground, the player who struck it wins the point; if before it hits the ground his opponent wins the point.

22.　It is a good return:

(a) If the ball touch the net, posts, cord or metal cable, strap or band, provided that it passes over any of them and hits the ground within the Court; or

(b) If the ball, served or returned, hit the ground within the proper court and rebound or be blown back over the net, and the player whose turn it is to strike reach over the net and play the ball, provided that neither he nor any part of his clothes or racket touch the net, posts, cord or metal cable, strap or band or the ground within his opponent's court, and that the stroke be otherwise good; or

(c) If the ball be returned outside the post, either above or below the level of the top of the net, even though it touch the post, provided that it hits the ground within the proper Court; or

(d) If a player's racket pass over the net after he has returned the ball, provided the ball pass the net before being played and be properly returned; or

(e) If a player succeeds in returning the ball, served or in play, which strikes a ball lying in the Court.

NOTE TO RULE 22—In a singles match, if, for the sake of convenience a doubles Court be equipped with singles posts for the purpose of a singles game,

then the doubles posts and those portions of the net, cord or metal cable and band outside such singles posts shall at all times be permanent fixtures, and are not regarded as posts or parts of the net of a singles game.

A return that passes under the net cord between the singles and adjacent doubles post without touching either net cord, net or doubles post and falls within the area of play, is a good return.

23.　In case a player is hindered in making a stroke by anything not within his control, except a permanent fixture of the Court, or except as provided for in Rule 19, a let shall be called.

24.　If a player wins his first point, the score is called 15 for that player; on winning his second point, the score is called 30 for that player: on winning his third point, the score is called 40 for that player, and the fourth point won by a player is scored game for that player except as below:

If both players have won three points, the score is called deuce; and the next point won by a player is scored advantage for that player. If the same player win the next point, he wins the game; if the other player wins the next point the score is again called deuce; and so on, until a player wins the two points immediately following the score at deuce, when the game is scored for that player.

25.　A player (or players) who first wins six games wins a set; except that he must win by a margin of two games over his opponent, and, where necessary, a set shall be extended until this margin be achieved.

26.　The players shall change sides at the end of the first, third and every subsequent alternate game of each set, and at the end of each set unless the total number of games in such set be even, in which case the change is not made until the end of the first game of the next set.

27.　The maximum number of sets in a match shall be 5, or, where women take part, 3.

28.　Except where otherwise stated, every reference in these Rules to the masculine includes the feminine gender.

Rule 29 of the Rules of Lawn Tennis, as amended by the International Lawn Tennis Federation on 7th July, 1971.

　　　In matches where an Umpire is appointed, his decision shall be final: but where a Referee is appointed, an appeal shall lie to him from the decision of an Umpire or a question of law, and in all such cases the decision of the Referee shall be final.

In matches where assistants to the Umpire are appointed (linesmen, net cord judges, foot-fault judges) their decisions shall be final on questions of fact.

When such an assistant is unable to give a decision he shall indicate this immediately to the Umpire who shall give a decision. When an Umpire is unable to give a decision on a question of fact he shall order a let to be called.

In Davis Cup matches only, the decision of an assistant to the Umpire, or of the Umpire if the assistant is unable to make a decision, can be changed by the Referee, who may also authorise the Umpire to change the decision of an assistant or order a let to be called.

The Referee, in his discretion, may at any time postpone a match on account of darkness or the condition of the ground or the weather. In any case of postponement the previous score and previous occupancy of Courts shall hold good, unless the Referee and the players unanimously agree otherwise.

30.   Play shall be continuous from the first service till the match be concluded; provided that after the third set, or when women take part, the second set, either player is entitled to a rest, which shall not exceed 10 minutes, or in countries situated between Latitude 15 degree North and Latitude 15 degrees South 45 minutes, and provided further that when necessitated by circumstances not within the control of the players, the Umpire may suspend play for such a period as he may consider necessary. If play be suspended and be not resumed until a later day the rest may be taken only after the third set (or when women take part, the second set) of play on such later day, completion of an unfinished set being counted as one set. These provisions shall be strictly construed, and play shall never be suspended, delayed or interfered with for the purpose of enabling a player to recover his strength or his wind, or to receive instruction or advice. The Umpire shall be the sole judge of such suspension, delay or interference, and after giving due warning he may disqualify the offender.

NOTE—Any nation is at liberty to modify the first provision in Rule 30 or omit it from its regulations governing tournaments, matches or competitions held in its own country, other than the International Lawn Tennis Championships (Davis Cup and Federation Cup).

When changing sides a maximum of one minute shall elapse from the cessation of the previous game to the time players are ready to begin the next game.

THE DOUBLES GAME

31.   The above Rules shall apply to the Doubles Game except as below.

32.   For the Doubles Game, the Court shall be 36 feet (10.97m.) in width, i.e., 4½ feet (1.37m.) wider on each side than the Court for the Singles Game, and those portions of the singles side-lines which lie between the two service-lines shall be called the service-side-lines. In other respects, the Court shall be similar to that described in Rule 1, but the portions of the singles side-lines between the base-line and service-line on each side of the net may be omitted if desired.

33.   The order of serving shall be decided at the beginning of each set as follows:

The pair who have to serve in the first game of each set shall decide which partner shall do so and the opposing pair shall decide similarly for the second game. The partner of the player who served in the first game shall serve in the third; the partner of the player who served in the second game shall serve in the fourth, and so on in the same order in all the subsequent games of a set.

34.   The order of receiving a service shall be decided at the beginning of each set as follows:

The pair who have to receive the service in the first game shall decide which partner shall receive the first service, and that partner shall continue to receive the first service in every odd game throughout that set. The opposing pair shall likewise decide which partner shall receive the first service in the second game and that partner shall continue to receive the first service in every even game throughout that set. Partners shall receive the service alternately throughout each game.

35.   If a partner serve out of his turn, the partner who ought to have served shall serve as soon as the mistake is discovered, but all points scored, and any faults served before such discovery, shall be reckoned. If a game shall have been completed before such discovery, the order of service remains as altered.

36.   If during a game the order of receiving the service is changed by the receivers it shall remain as altered until the end of the game in which the mistake is discovered, but the partners shall resume their original order of receiving in the next game of that set in which they are receivers of the service.

37.   The service is a fault as provided for by Rule 9, or if the ball touch the Server's partner or anything which he wears or carries; but if the ball served touch the partner of the Receiver, or anything which he wears or carries, not being a let under Rule 13 (a) before it hits the ground, the Server wins the point.

38.   The ball shall be struck alternately by one or other player of the opposing pairs, and if a player touches the ball in play with his racket in contravention of this Rule, his opponents win the point.

Questions on the Rules

1. May a player reach over the net with his racket and play a stroke ?

2. May a player hit the ball around (i.e., outside) the post and into court ?

3. A service strikes the top of the net post and goes into the correct court. Is it a let or fault ?

4. May the server in a Singles serve from behind that part of the base-line which is at the back of the Doubles Side-lines?

5. In Handicap Matches, does the server start serving into the right court regardless of the handicap ?

6. A player throws the ball up to serve but decides not to strike it, and catches the ball in his hand or on his racket. Is it a fault ?

7. If a player serves a fault when serving from the wrong court and then discovers his error, what is the procedure ?

8. A player serves from the wrong court and the mistake is discovered after the point is completed. Does the point stand and from which court is the next service delivered ?

9. A ball in play strikes a ball lying on the court. Should a let be played ?

10. The spectators at a match are sitting so close to the court that a player is prevented from making his stroke. May he claim a replay ?

11. The ball goes into the net, but the player on the other side, thinking the ball is coming over, makes a stroke and touches the net. Whose point is it ?

12. The receiver is standing outside the Service Court and is struck by a service ball before the ball has struck the ground. Is this service a fault ?

13. In a doubles game, the ball served hits the receiver's partner before touching the ground. Who scores the point?

14. If the Umpire calls a replay because a spectator has hampered a player, or because a ball has rolled on court during a rally, is the server entitled to one more service or two ?

15. May the server in a Doubles Game stand anywhere behind the Doubles base-line provided he is on the correct side of the centre mark ?

16. May the server's partner stand anywhere at the net even if he obscures the view of the receiver ?

17. A player standing outside the base-line is hit by a ball or catches it before it bounces. Who scores the point ?

18. In a Doubles Game the score is 40/15 when it is discovered that the wrong player is serving. Should he continue serving until the game is concluded ?

19. If it is discovered during a Doubles Game that the receivers are in the wrong courts, should they change immediately to the correct ones ?

20. The receiver is struck by a service ball which has not hit the ground, but which has hit the top of the net in passing over it. Whose point is it ?

21. Is a player liable to a penalty if in making a stroke he touches his opponent ?

22. A return hits the Umpire or his chair or stand. The player claims that the ball was going into court. Whose point is it?

23. May a player jump over the net into his opponent's court while the ball is in play and not suffer penalty?

24. If an Umpire or other judge erroneously calls "fault" or "out" and then corrects himself, which of the calls shall prevail?

Answers to Questions

1. Yes, provided the ball has bounced on his side of the net and screwed (or been blown) back into his opponent's court. No, if it has not passed over the net prior to his stroke.

2. Yes, the stroke counts even if the ball touches the post, except from a service.

3. It is a fault.

4. No.

5. Yes.

6. No, he has not attempted to hit the ball.

7. The fault counts and he must serve the second service from the correct court.

8. The point stands and the next service is made from the same court.

9. No, it is up to the player on whose side the ball is lying to clear the ball away before a point is played.

10. No, the seating accommodation of the spectators is part of the general arrangements and is a "permanent fixture." If, however, a spectator were to stretch out his arm and so interfere with the player, a replay should be called.

11. The player who put the ball into the net wins the point if his opponent hit the net whilst the ball was still in play, i.e., before it hit the net.

12. No, the receiver loses the point.

13. The receiver loses the point.

14. Two. If a replay is called during the rally, the whole point is replayed and any previous fault is annulled.

15. Yes, provided that he is between the continuation of the centre mark and the outer side-line.

16. Yes.

17. His opponent.

18. No, the correct server must take over as soon as the mistake is discovered.

19. No, they must play out the game in the wrong courts but change in the next receiving game.

20. The service is a let.

21. No, unless the Umpire considers it necessary to take action under Rule 19.

22. He loses the point.

23. No, he loses the point, see Rule 18 (e).

24. A let must be called unless in the opinion of the Umpire, neither player is hindered in his game, in which case the corrected call shall prevail.

Making a Draw

The name of each entry (that is player or doubles pair) is written on a separate card and placed in a hat together with all the others. The names are drawn out one by one at random and listed in the order in which they were drawn.

When the number of entries is exactly 4, 8, 16, 32, 64, etc., all the entries will compete in the first round and the winners of each round compete with the next winner in the list. After a certain number of rounds, depending upon the number of entries, there will be 2 players (or pairs) left to fight out the final. Example, 8 entries show:

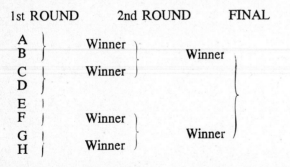

1st ROUND   2nd ROUND   FINAL

A
B — Winner
C
D — Winner   Winner
E
F — Winner
G
H — Winner   Winner

Where the number of entries is not exactly 4, 8, 16, 32, 64, etc., it is necessary to give a certain number of players "byes" so that the entries in second round will be exactly 4, 8, 16, 32 or 64.

POSITION OF BYES

The byes are placed at the top and bottom of the draw, divided equally, and if there is an odd number of byes one more bye is placed in the bottom. The first names out of the hat will be given byes in the top half, and the last will be given byes in the lower half. All the other entries will compete in the first round. Examples of 11 entries. $16 — 11 = 5$, so there will be 5 byes.

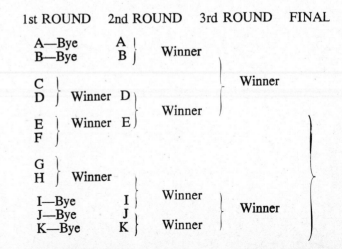

1st ROUND   2nd ROUND   3rd ROUND   FINAL

A—Bye   A
B—Bye   B   Winner
C
D — Winner D
E — Winner E   Winner
F
G
H — Winner
I—Bye   I
J—Bye   J — Winner   Winner
K—Bye   K — Winner

Printed in Great Britain by Sunstreet Printing Works (Keighley) Ltd.